GEARING UP FOR SPORTS!

HOCKEY GEAR

NOAH RICCARDI

PowerKiDS press

Published in 2027 by The Rosen Publishing Group, Inc.
2544 Clinton Street, Buffalo, NY 14224

First Edition

Book Design: Madison Thogmartin

Photo Credits: Cover, p. 1 Dusan Petkovic/Shutterstock.com; p. 5 FotoDuets/Shutterstock.com; p. 7 Vladimir Vasiltvich/Shutterstock.com; p. 9 Iurii Osadchi/Shutterstock.com; p. 11 Vitalii Vitleo/Shutterstock.com; pp. 13, 21 GTS Productions/Shutterstock.com; p. 15 Tolmachov Vision/Shutterstock.com; p. 17 Jai Agnish/Shutterstock.com; p. 19 Lorraine Swanson/Shutterstock.com.

Cataloging-in-Publication Data
Names: Riccardi, Noah.
Title: Hockey gear / Noah Riccardi.
Description: Buffalo, New York : PowerKids Press, 2027. | Series: Gearing up for sports! | Includes glossary and index.
Identifiers: ISBN 9781499456707 (pbk.) | ISBN 9781499456714 (library bound) | ISBN 9781499456721 (ebook)
Subjects: LCSH: Hockey--Juvenile literature. | Hockey--Equipment and supplies--Juvenile literature.
Classification: LCC GV847.25 R533 2027 | DDC 796.962--dc23

Manufactured in China

CPSIA Compliance Information: Batch #QS27PK. For Further Information contact Rosen Publishing, at 1-800-237-9932.

CONTENTS

The Puck 4

Hockey Jersey 8

The Stick 10

Hockey Skates 14

Helmet and Pads 18

Goaltender Gear 20

Glossary 22

For More Information 23

Index 24

The Puck

The **object** of hockey is to get the puck into the goal. The puck is a **cylinder** that is 1 inch (2.5 cm) tall and 3 inches (7.6 cm) across. It is made of hard rubber. It slides easily across the ice.

Players hit the puck around a **rink**. Sometimes, the puck flies over the rink's walls. When this happens, play stops. Play starts again with a faceoff. This is when a **referee** drops the puck between two players.

ГАЗПРОМ
EASTON
BAUER
CCM

Hockey Jersey

Hockey players wear long-sleeved jerseys. Teams wear different colors. This lets players know who is on their team. Jerseys also have player names and numbers on the back. This helps people know who is who on the ice.

68
68
HANDZUS
26
26

The Stick

Players use sticks to control and hit the puck. The stick has a straight **shaft**. There is a curved **blade** on the end. The player holds the stick along the shaft. They play the puck using the blade.

TELUS
98
CANADA
SHERWOOD

Certain players on the ice use different types of sticks. Defenders use the longest sticks. Players on **offense** use slightly shorter sticks that help control the puck. Goaltender sticks are very short and wide to help block shots.

ITALIA
TRUE
HZRDUS
TRUE
TRUE
TRUE
L20.2
L20.2

Hockey Skates

Players use skates to move around the ice. Skates are like shoes with blades on the bottom. By using the edges of the blade, skaters can stop and turn on the slippery ice.

Skate blades are sharp. Players can get hurt if they crash or fall. So, players try to keep their blades near the ice and away from others. This keeps the game safe.

Newsday
17
Washington
Capitals
EASTON

Helmet and Pads

Hockey players sometimes crash into the rink's walls or each other. They wear a helmet and pads to protect themselves. Hockey helmets have a shield to protect the face. Pads cover the players' shoulders and chest.

22
10

Goaltender Gear

The goaltender's job is to block the puck. Players shoot the puck at high speeds. This means goaltenders need lots of protection. Goaltenders wear thick padding all over their body. They also wear a full helmet to protect their face.

35
TRUE
TRUE
TRUE

GLOSSARY

blade: The curved end of a hockey stick.

cylinder: A shape with flat, circular ends, and sides shaped like the outside of a tube.

object: The thing you are trying to do in a game.

offense: The part of the team that tries to score goals.

referee: Someone who makes sure players follow the rules of the game.

rink: An area of ice where a hockey game is played.

shaft: The long, straight part of a hockey stick.

FOR MORE INFORMATION

BOOKS

Abdo, Kenny. *Miracle Moments in Hockey*. Minneapolis, MN: Abdo Publishing, 2022.

Leed, Percy. *Hockey's Stanley Cup Finals*. Minneapolis, MN: Lerner Publications, 2025.

WEBSITES

NHL: Equipment
learntoplay.nhl.com/equipment/
Learn more about equipment for being rink-ready!

NHL & NHLPA: Learn to Play
learntoplay.nhl.com/
Learn more about the rules of hockey.

Publisher's note to educators and parents: Our editors have carefully reviewed these websites to ensure that they are suitable for students. Many websites change frequently, however, and we cannot guarantee that a site's future contents will continue to meet our high standards of quality and educational value. Be advised that students should be closely supervised whenever they access the internet.

INDEX

B
blades, 10, 14, 16

D
defenders, 12

G
goals, 4
goaltenders, 12, 20

H
helmets, 18, 20

I
ice, 4, 8, 12, 14, 16

J
jerseys, 8

O
offense, 12

P
pads, 18, 20
protection, 18, 20
pucks, 4, 6, 10, 12, 20

R
referees, 6
rinks, 6, 18
rubber, 4

S
shafts, 10
skates, 14, 16
sticks, 10, 12

W
walls, 6, 18